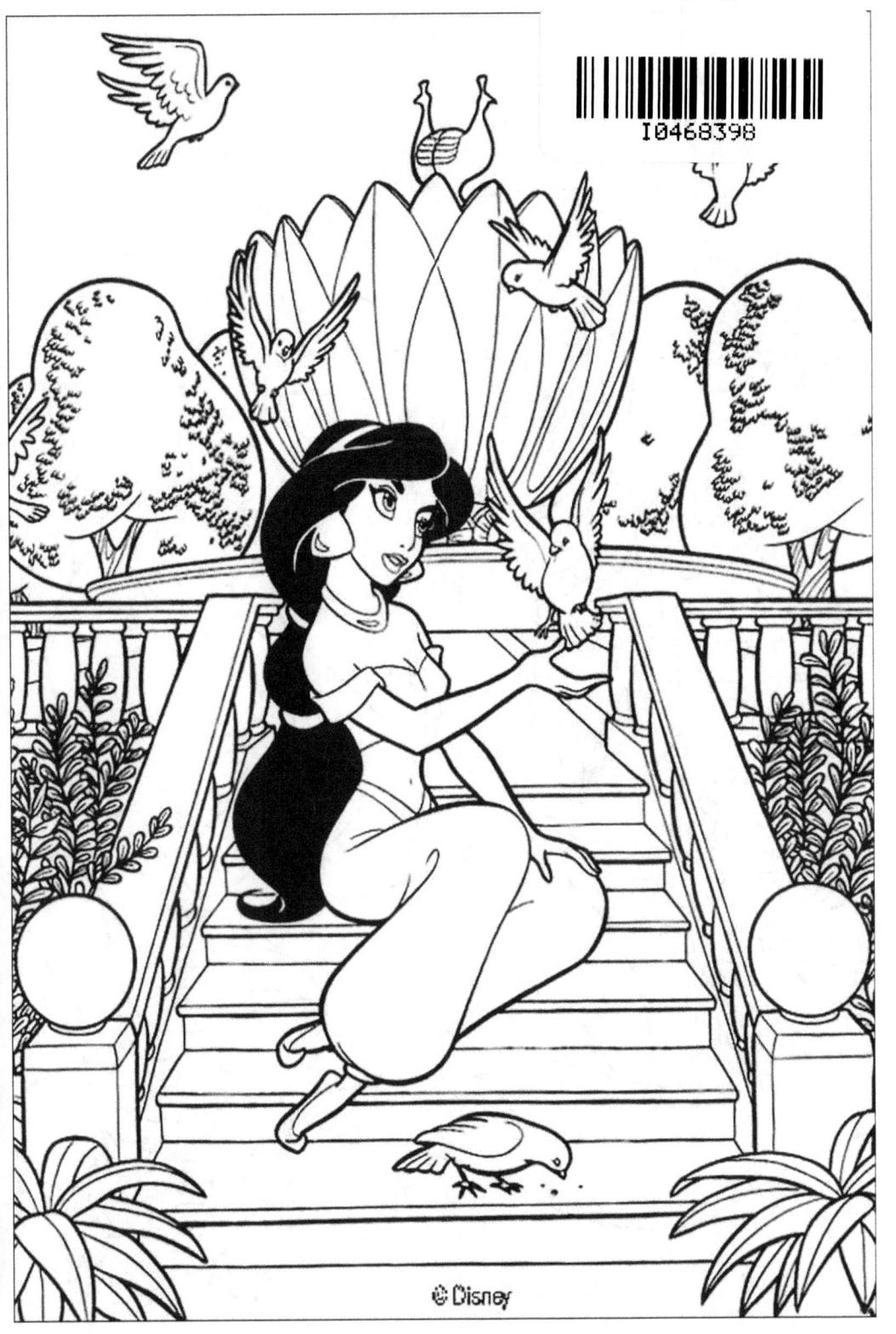

I0468398

© Disney

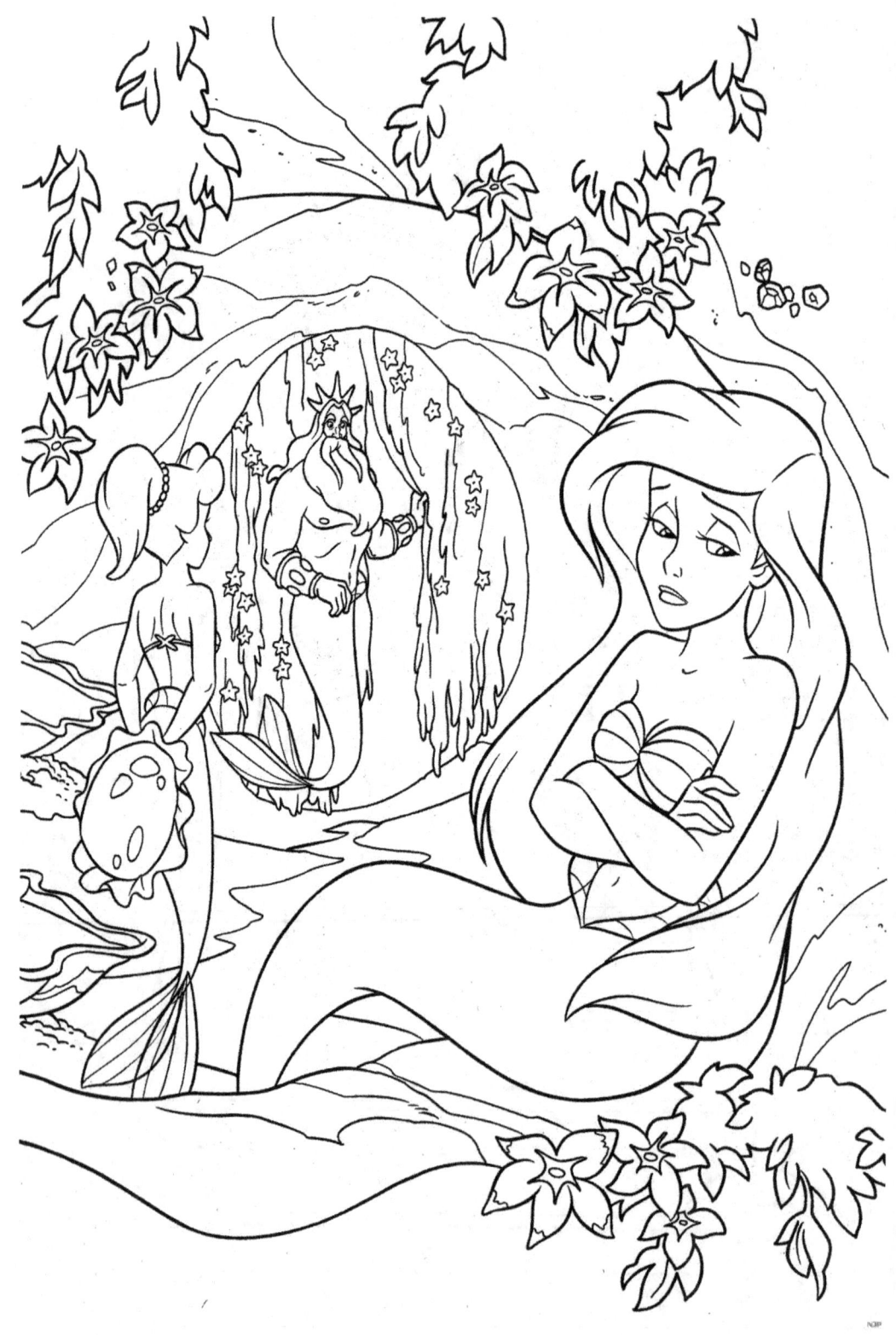

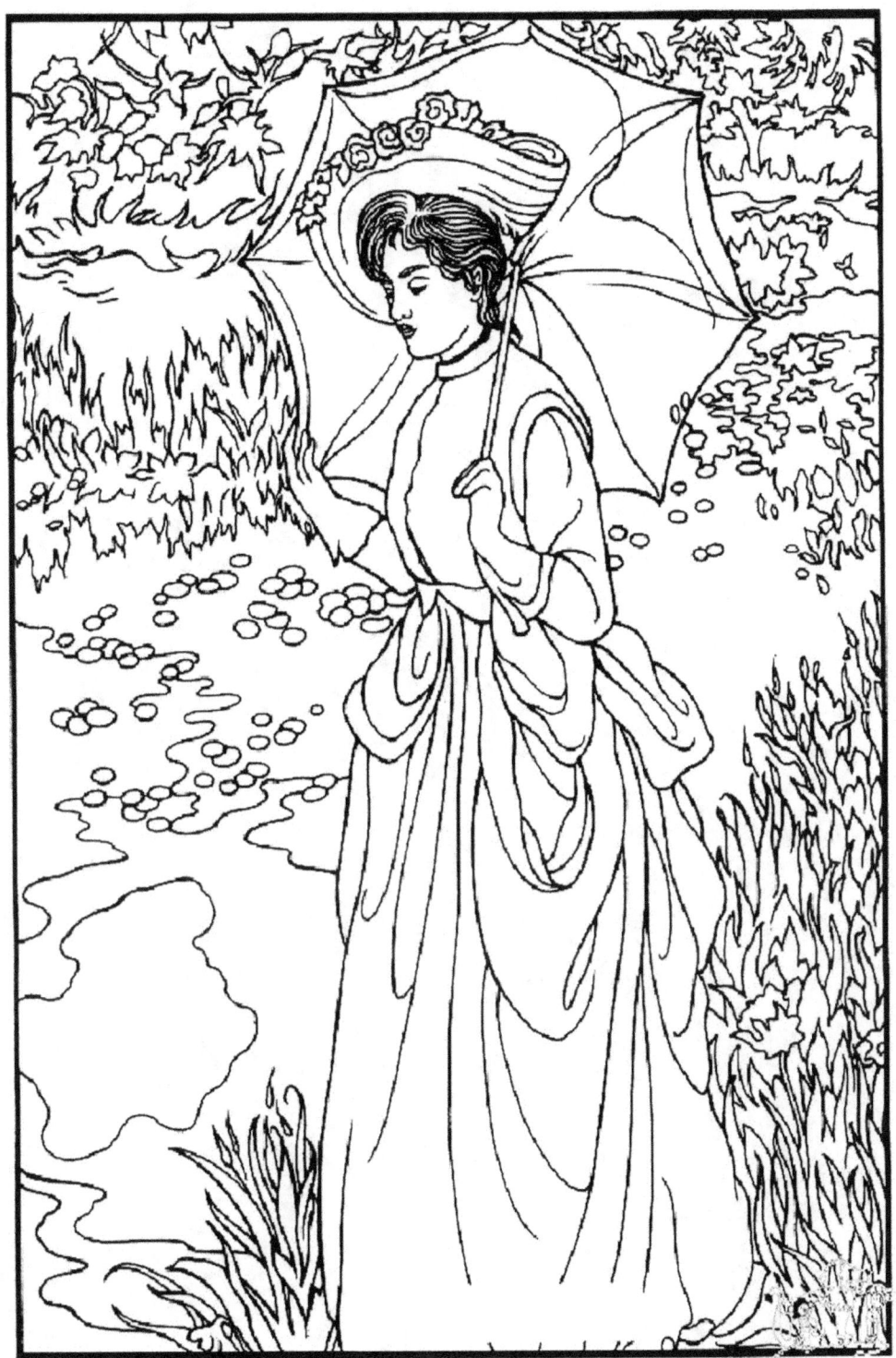

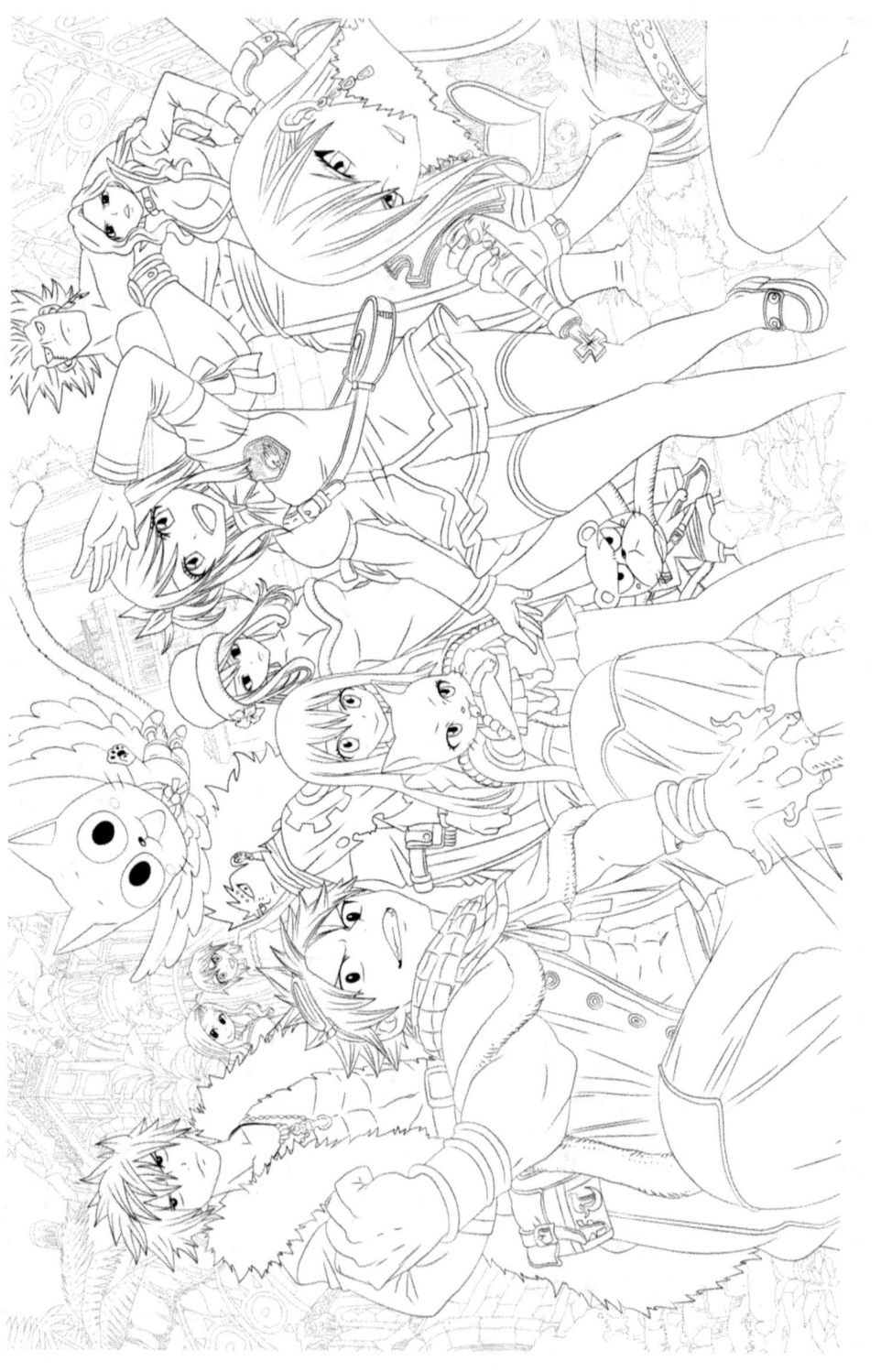

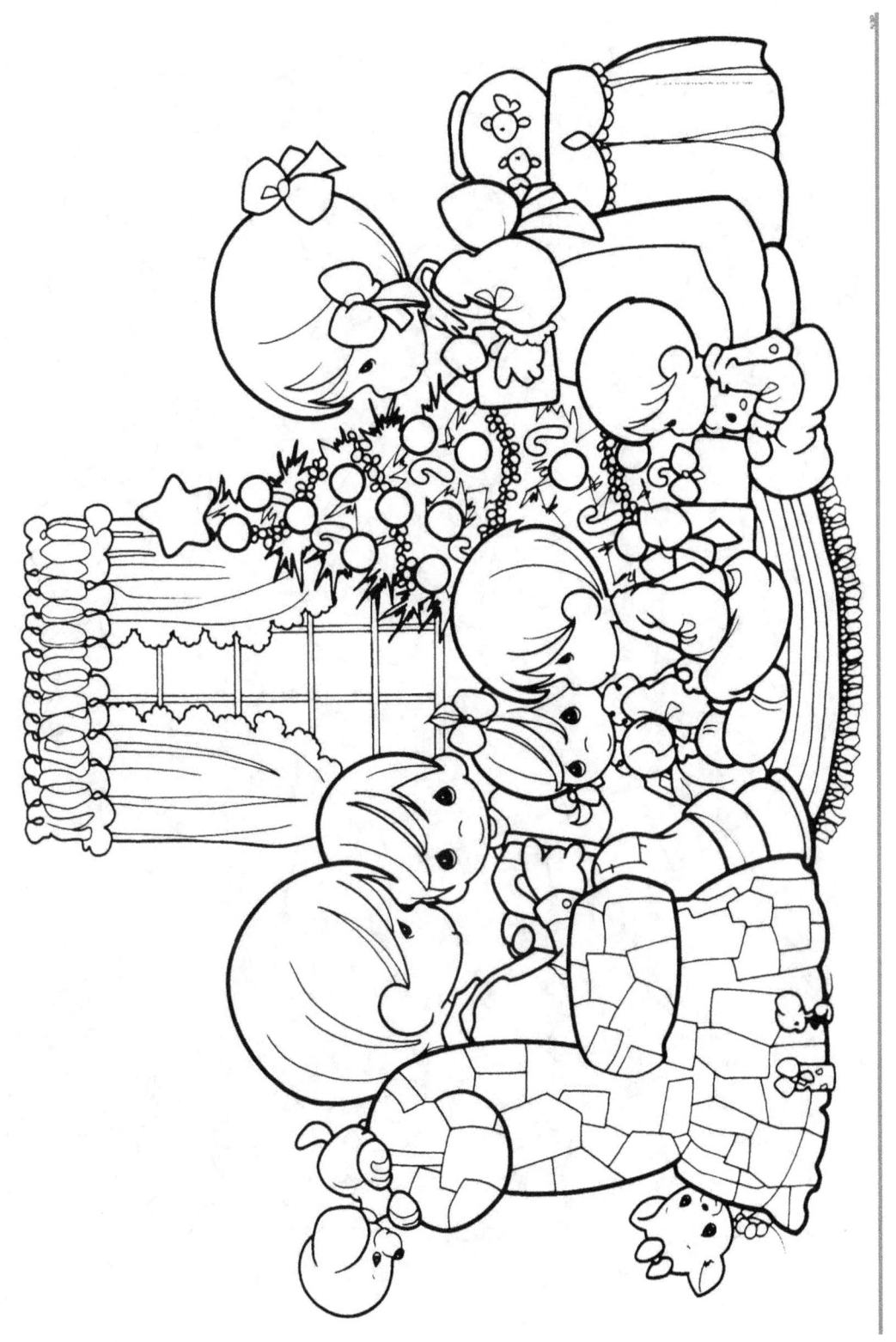

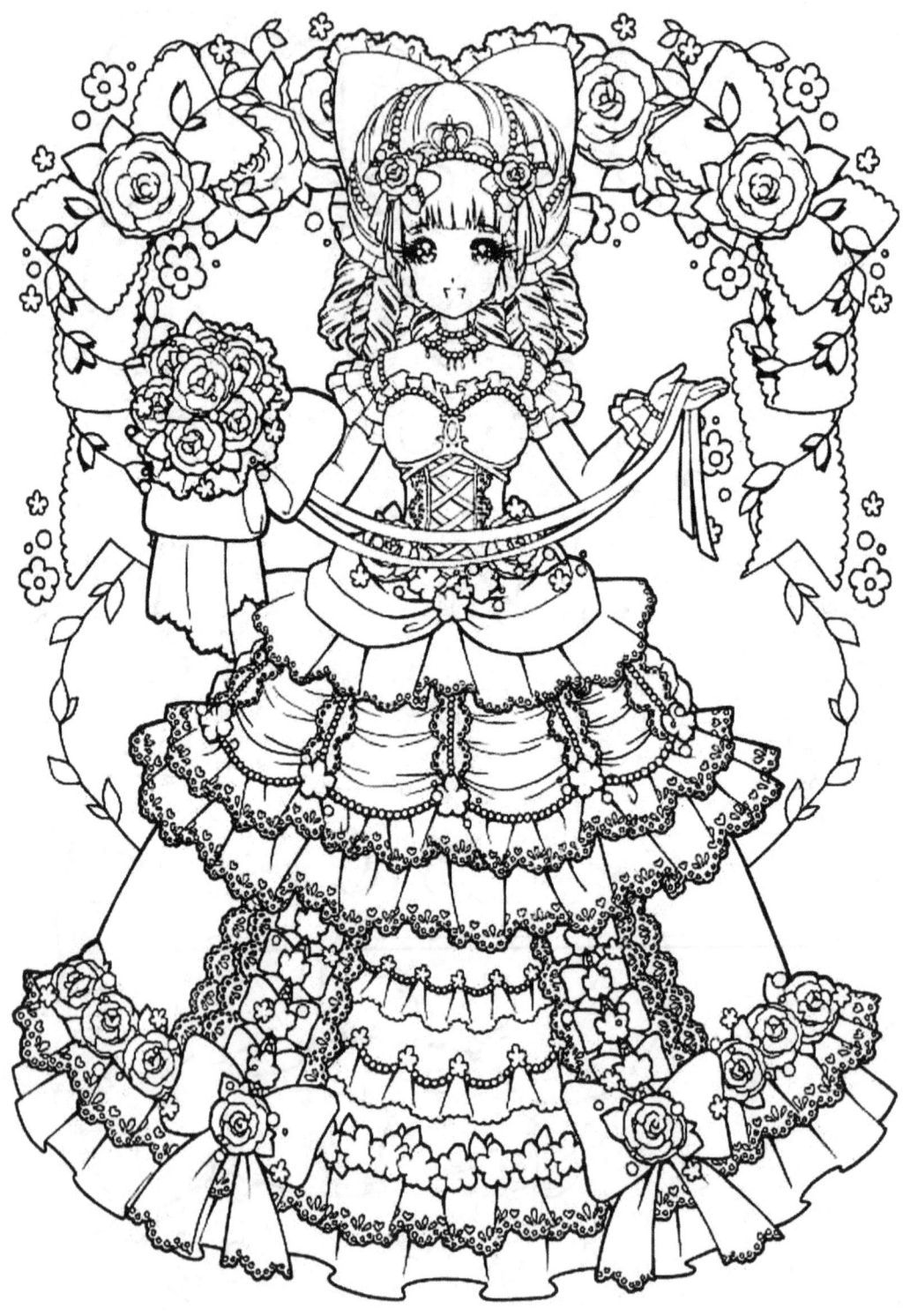

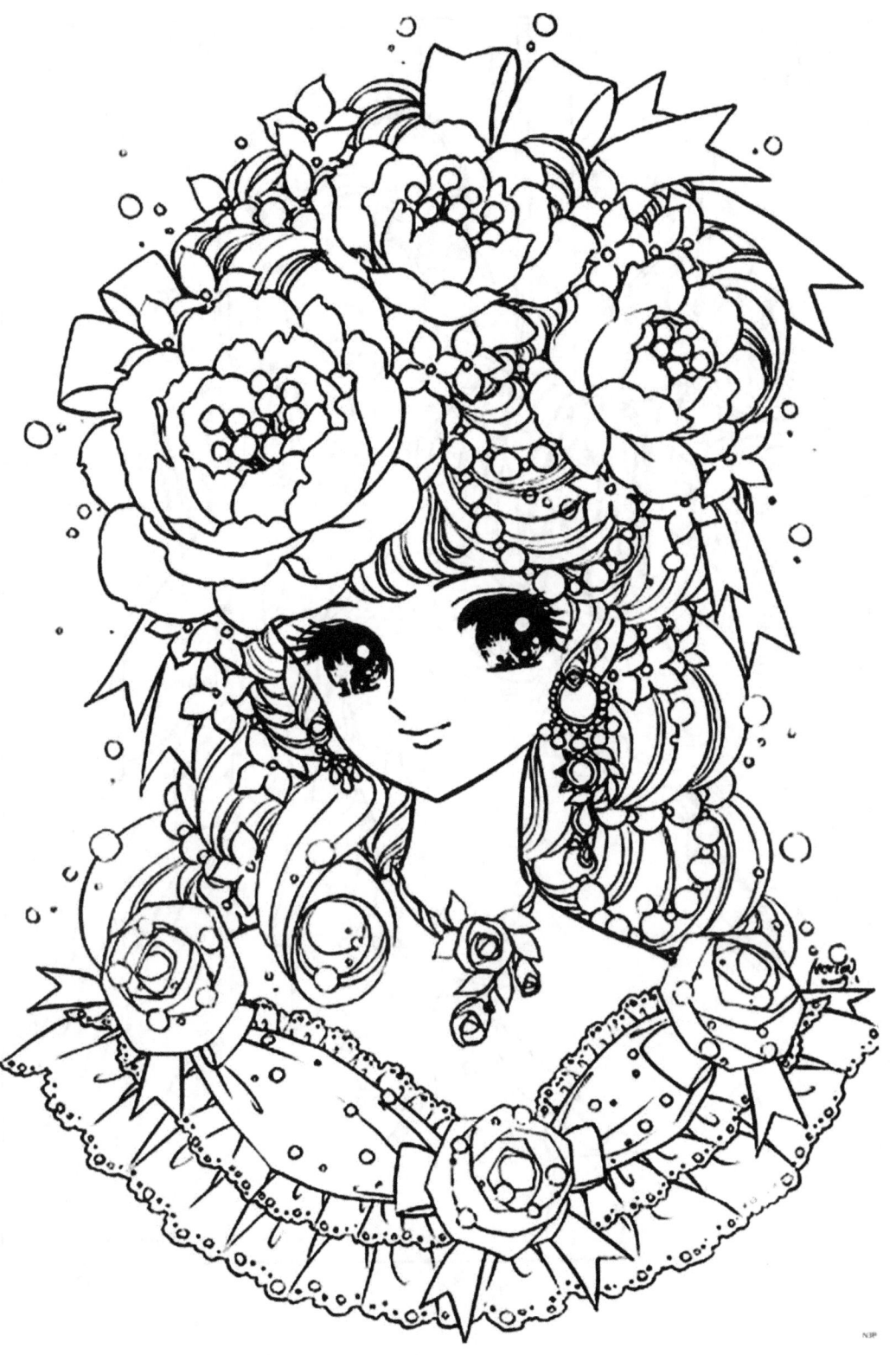

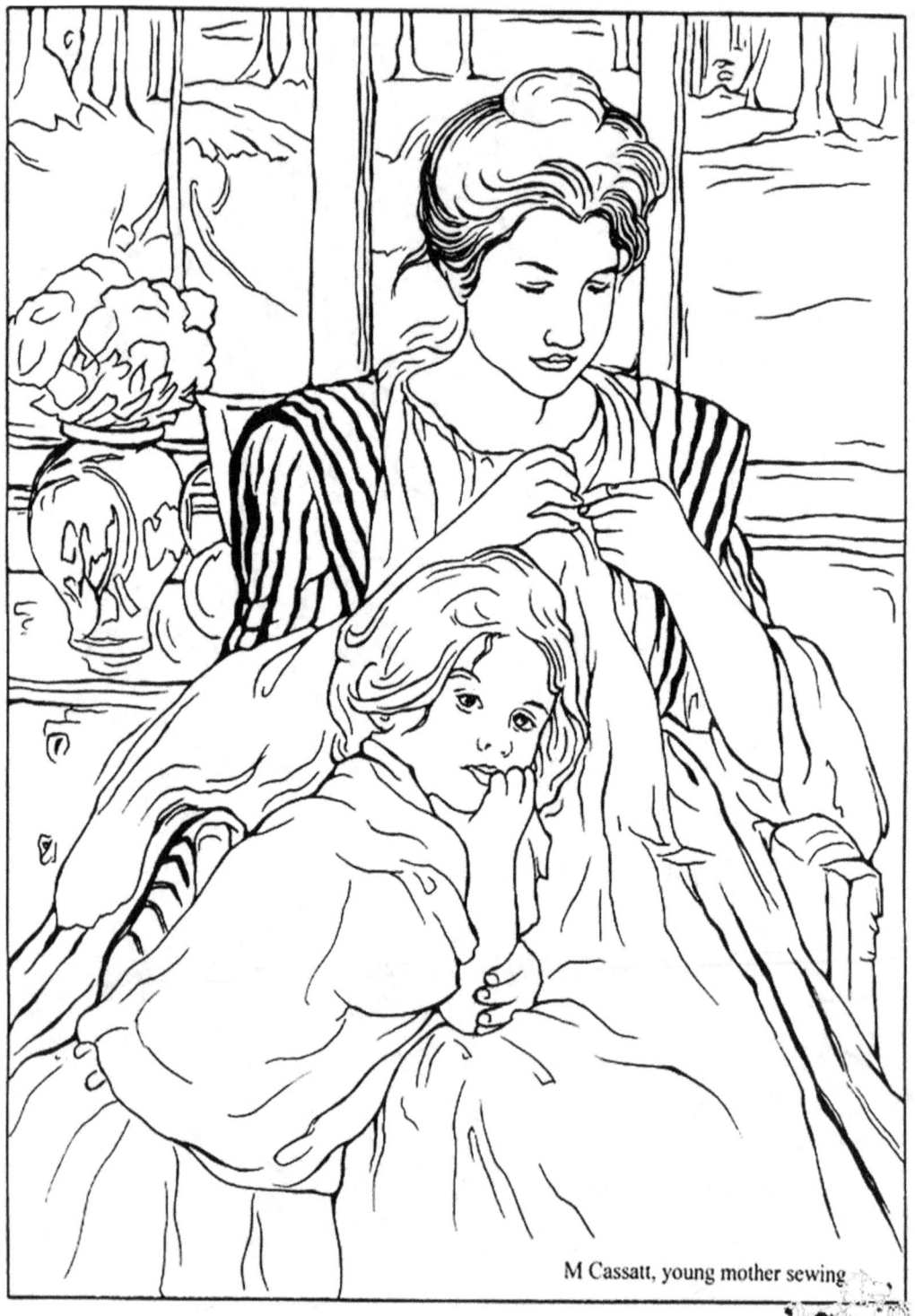

M Cassatt, young mother sewing

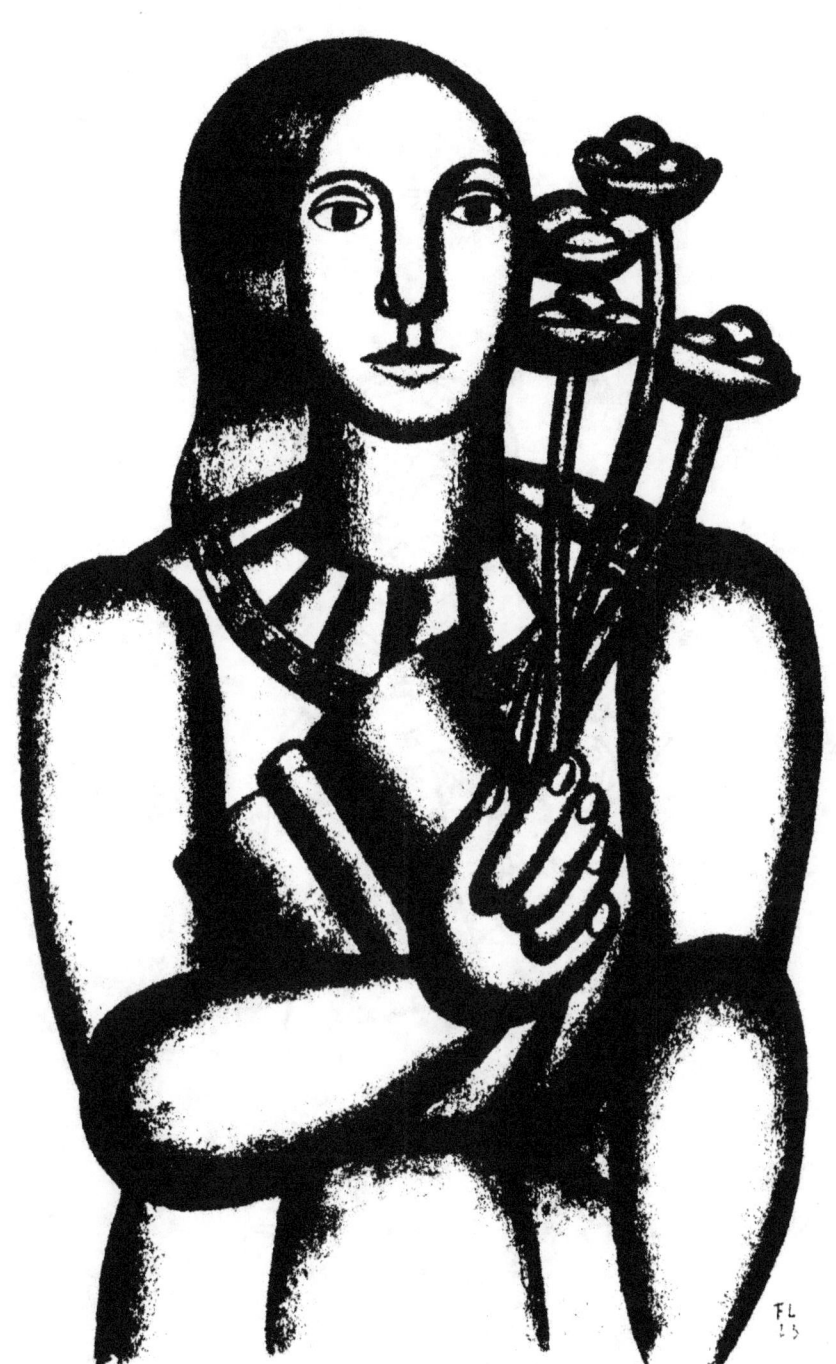

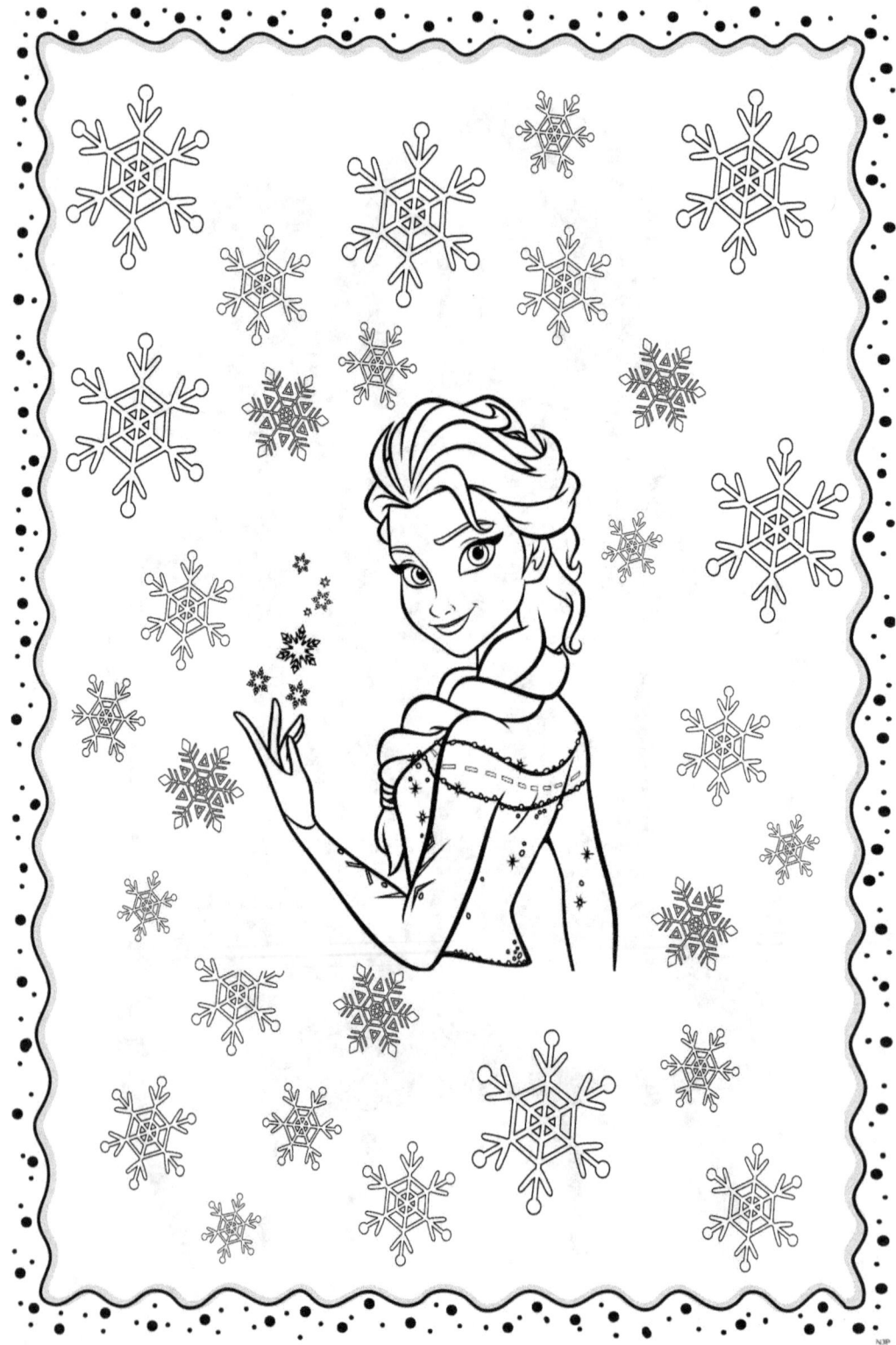

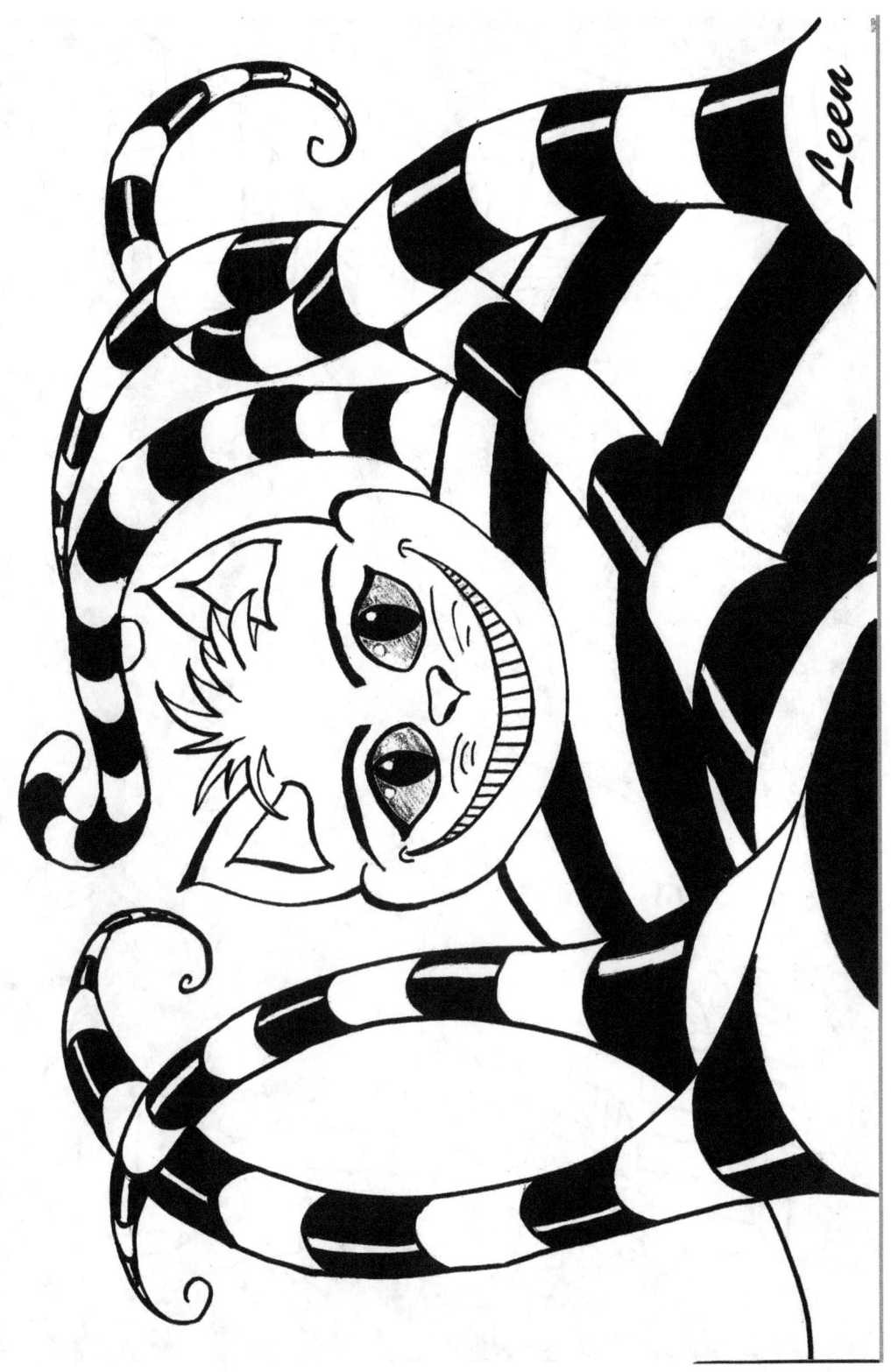

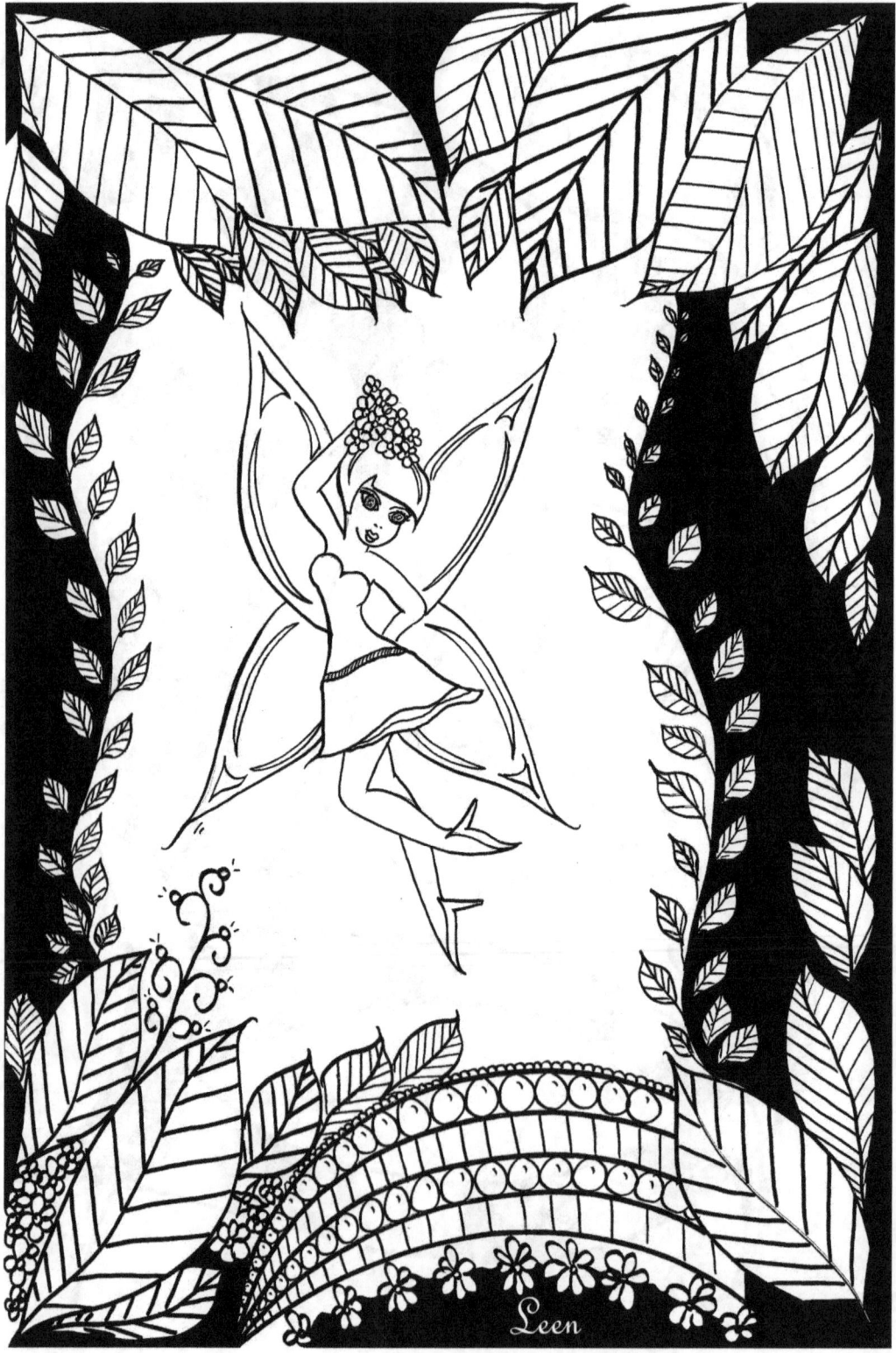

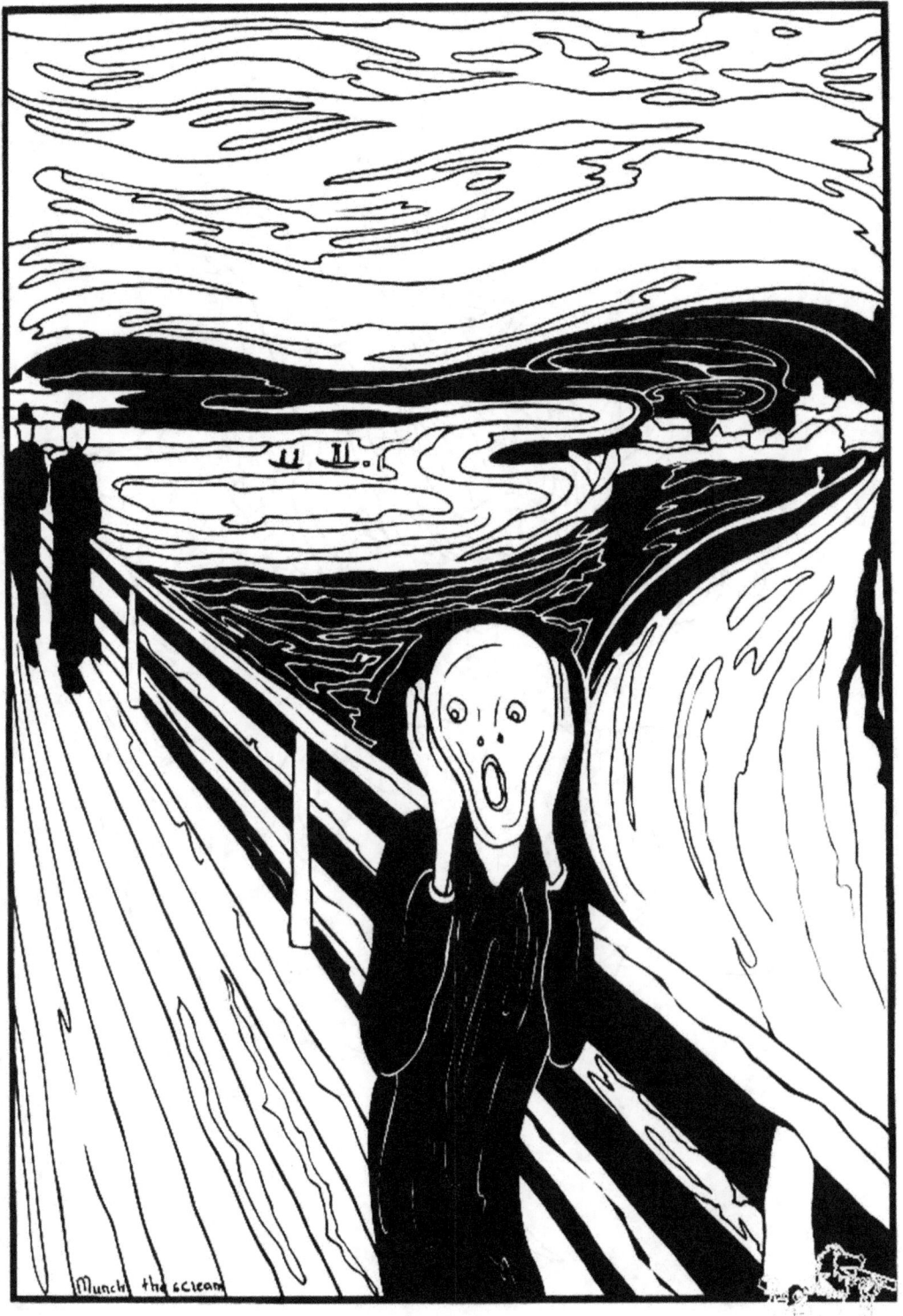

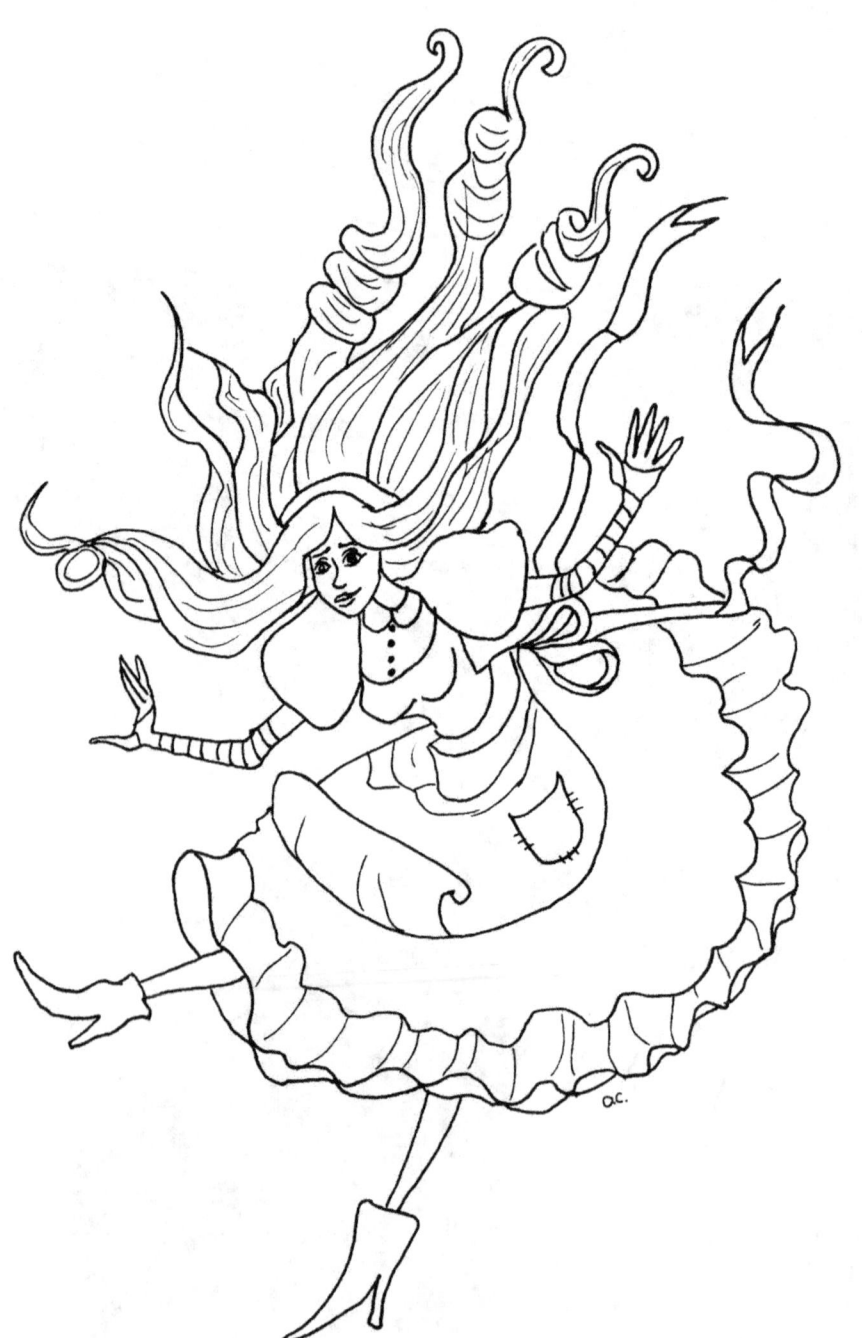

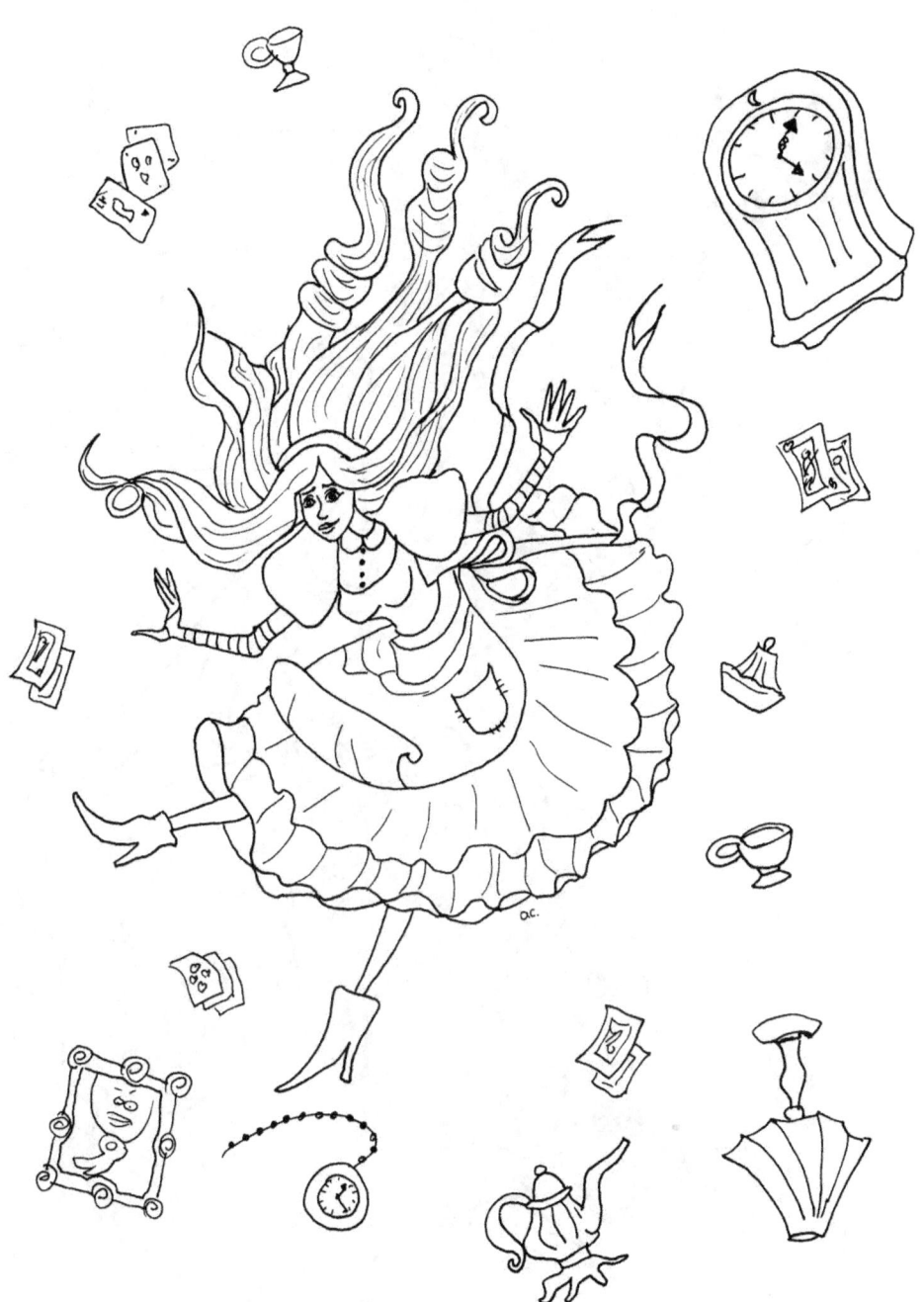

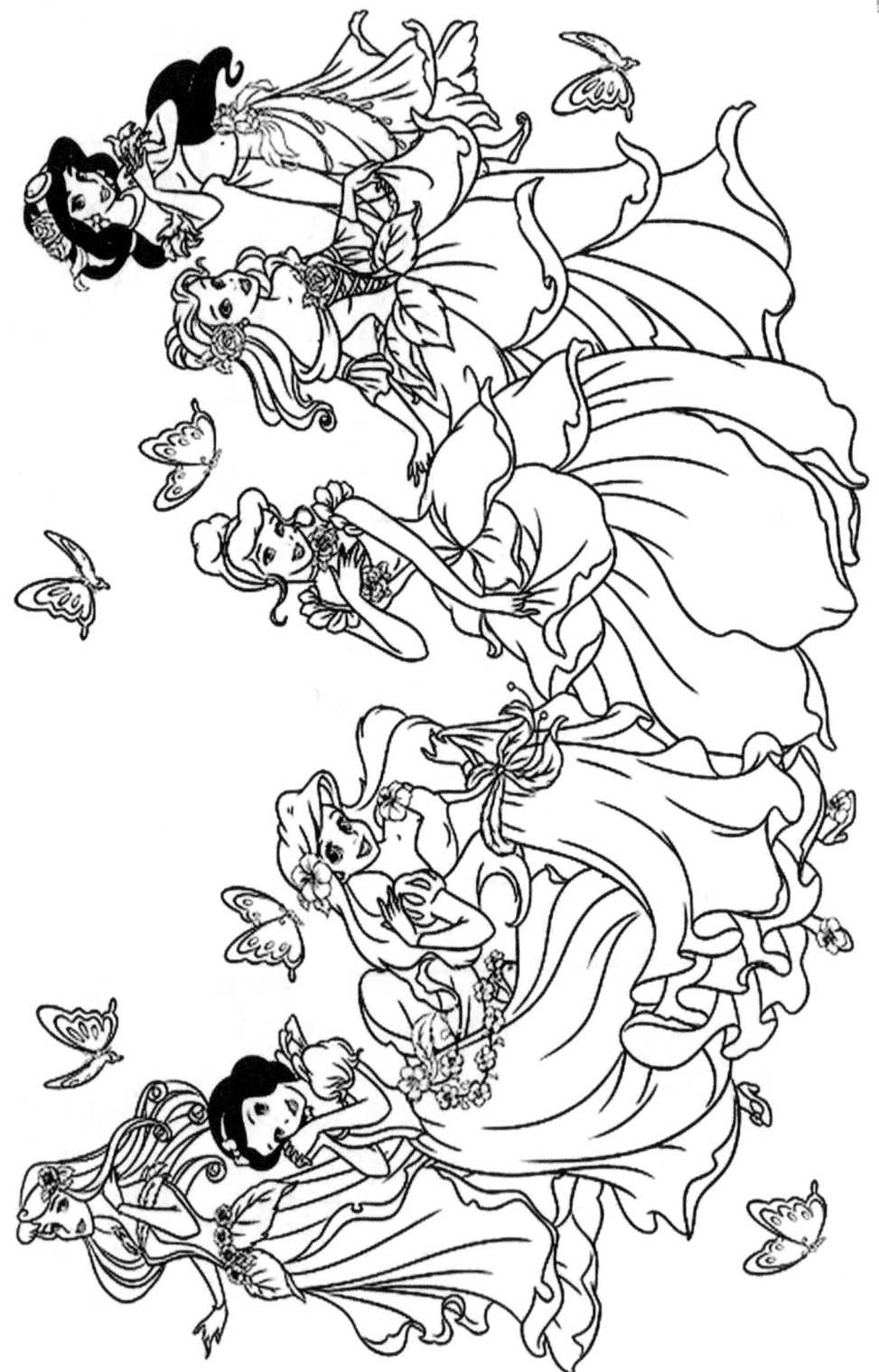

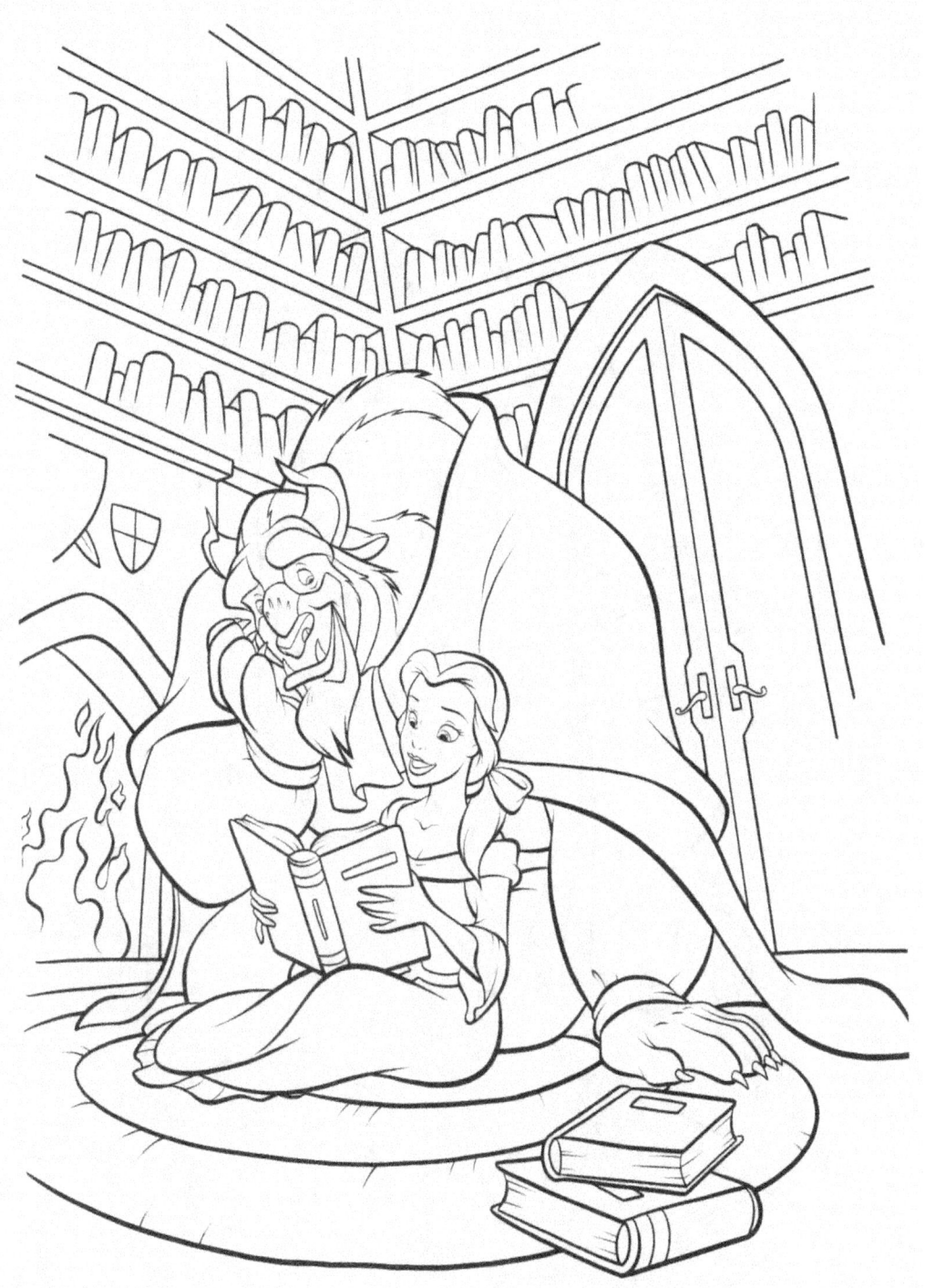

©Disney

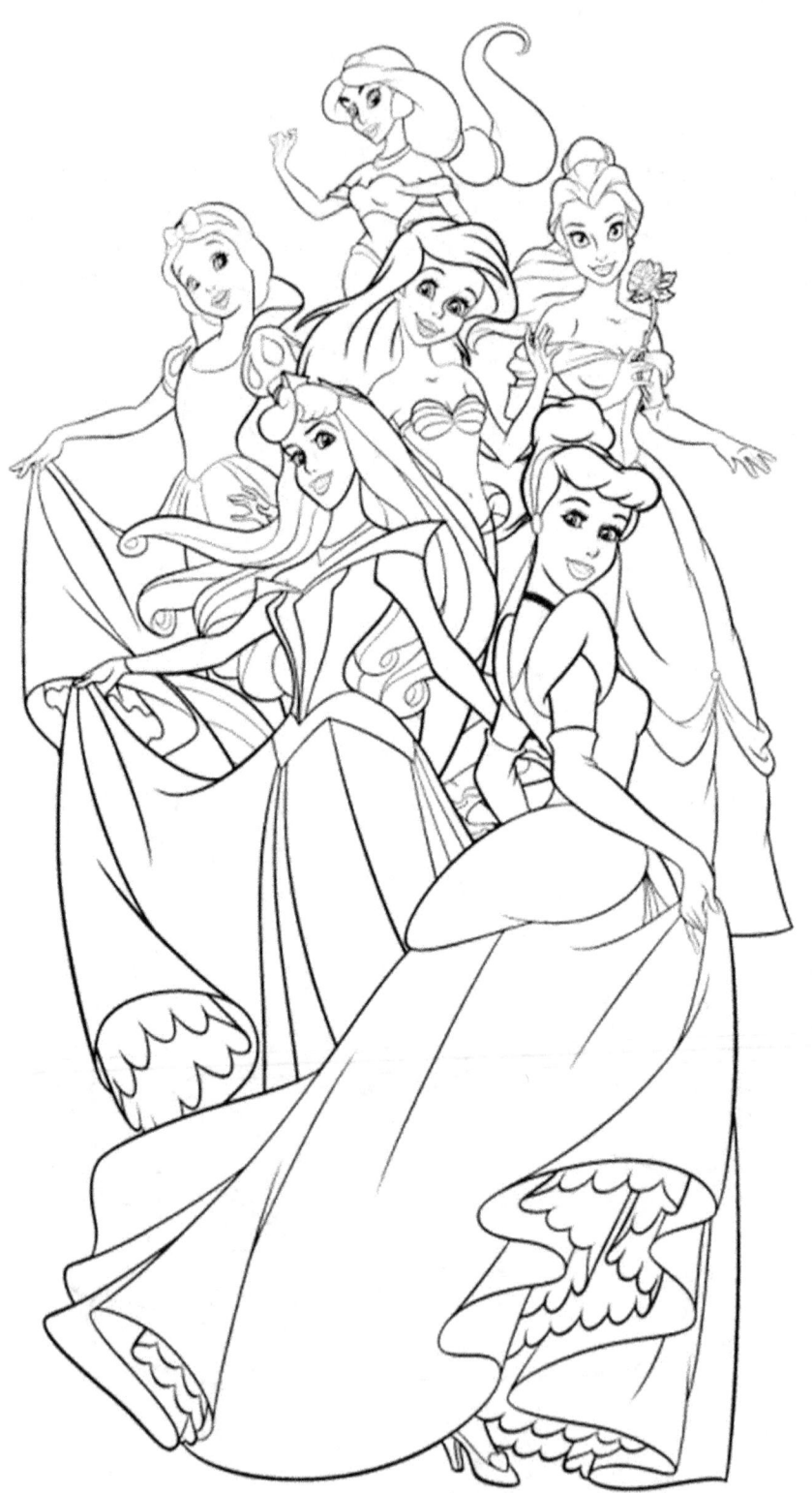

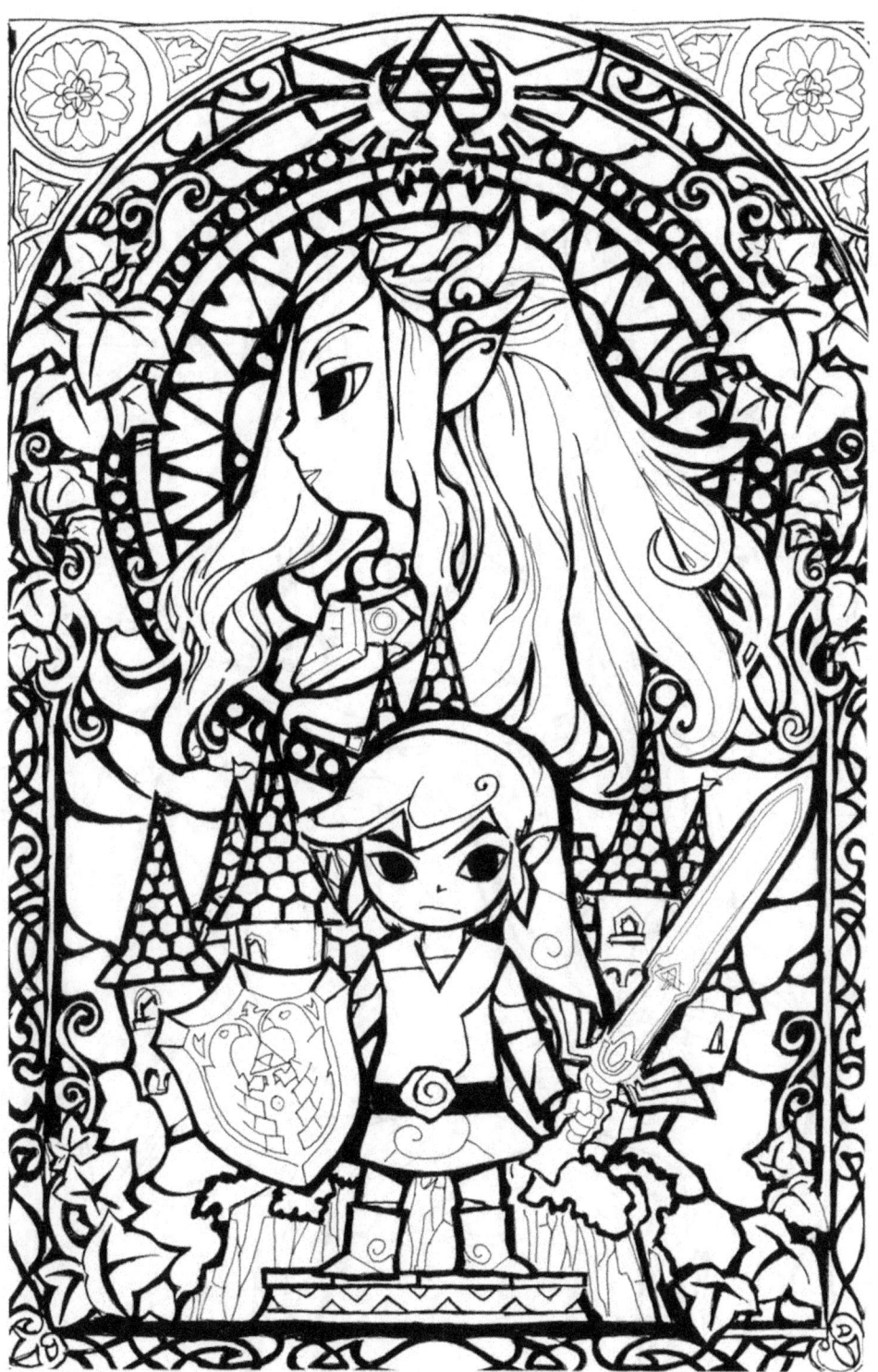

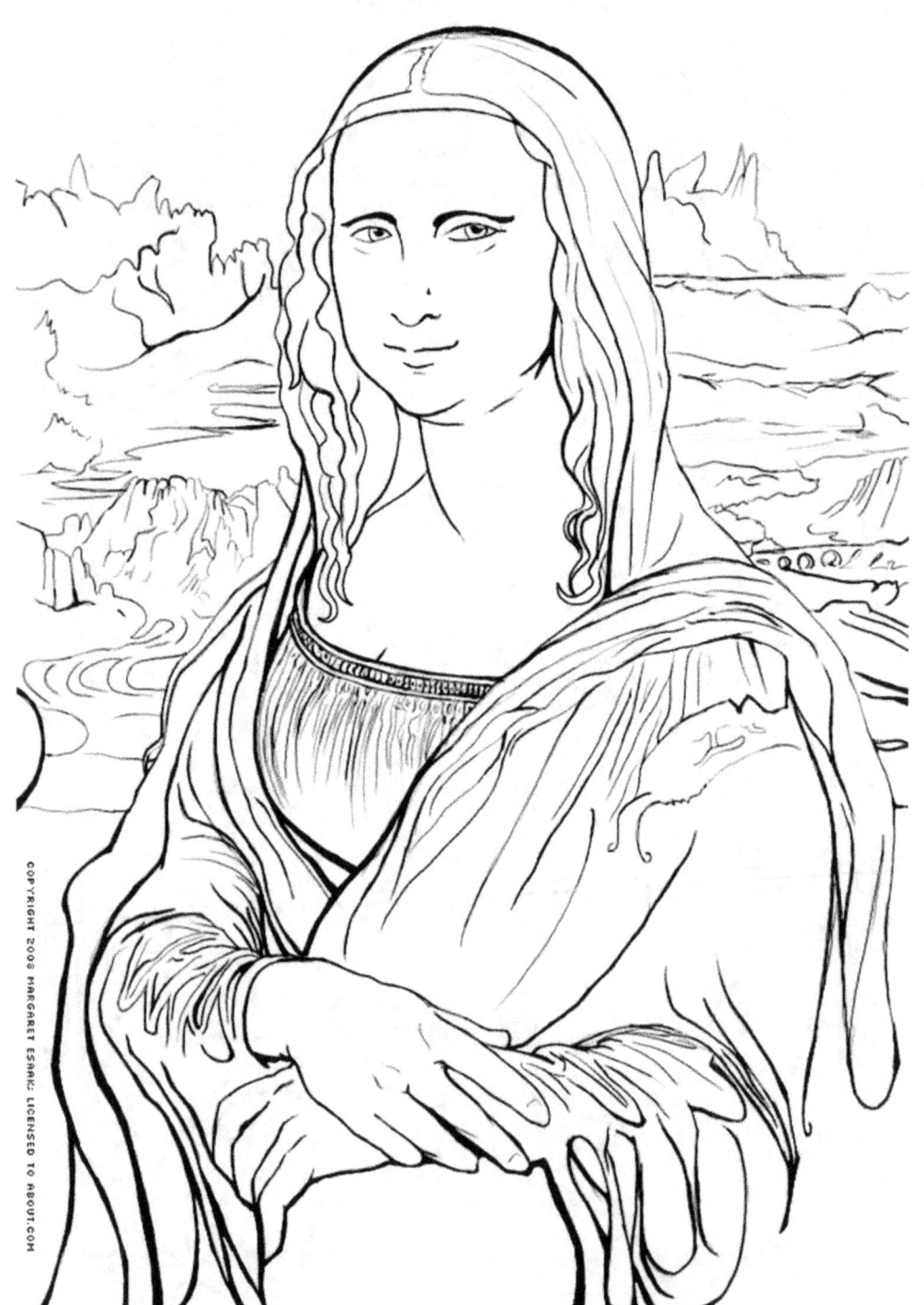

COPYRIGHT 2008 MARGARET ESAKI. LICENSED TO ABOUT.COM

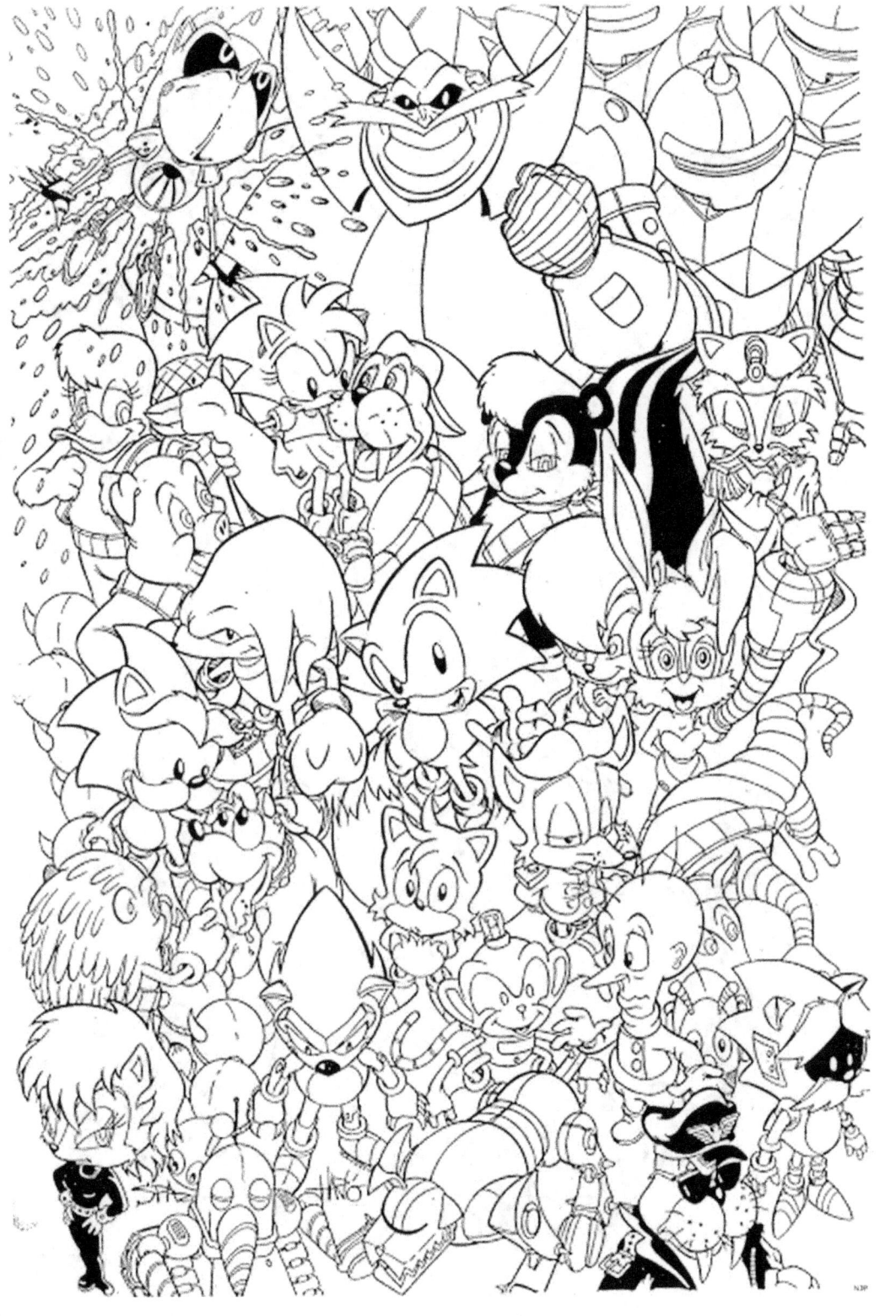

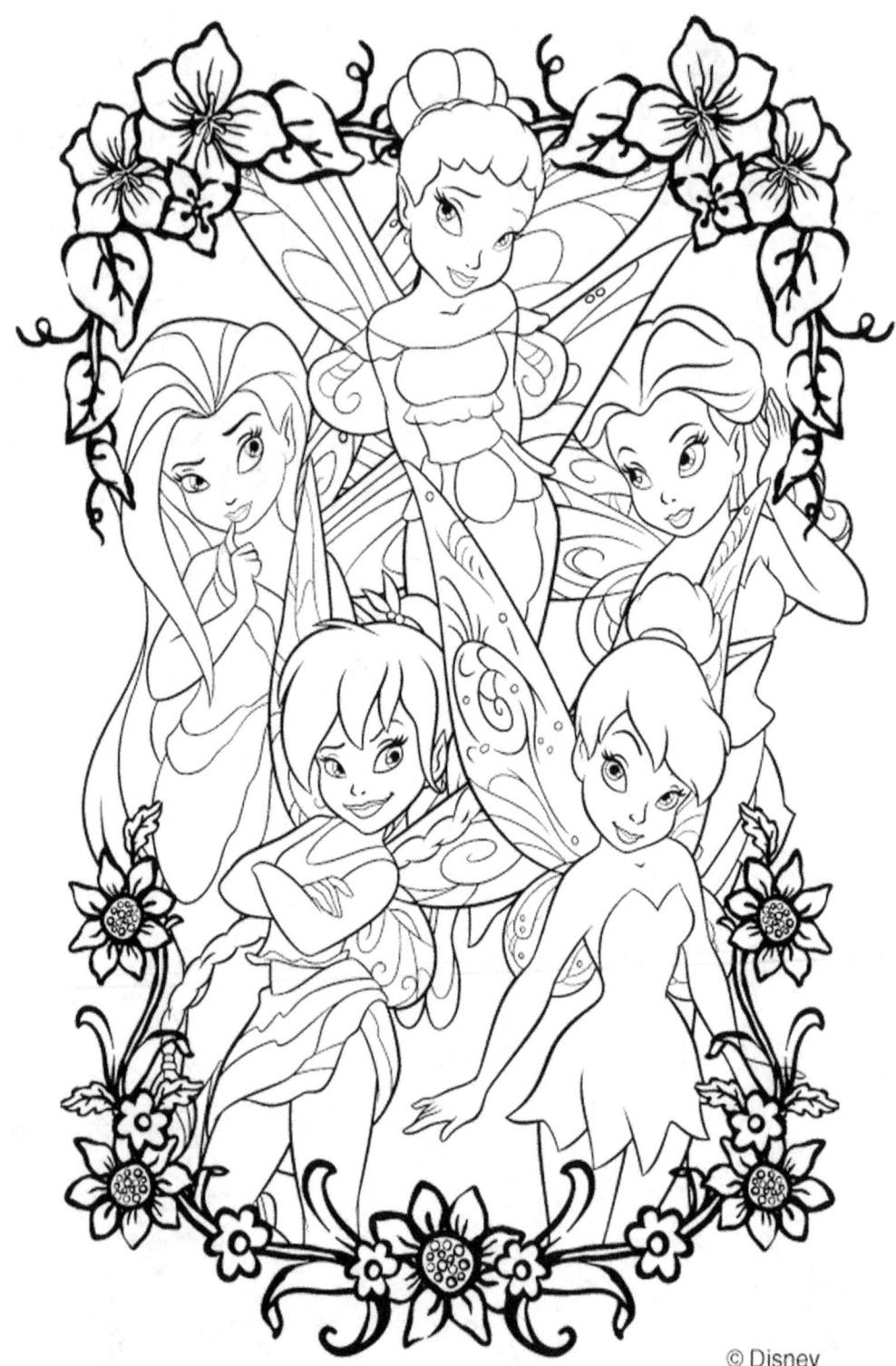

© Disney

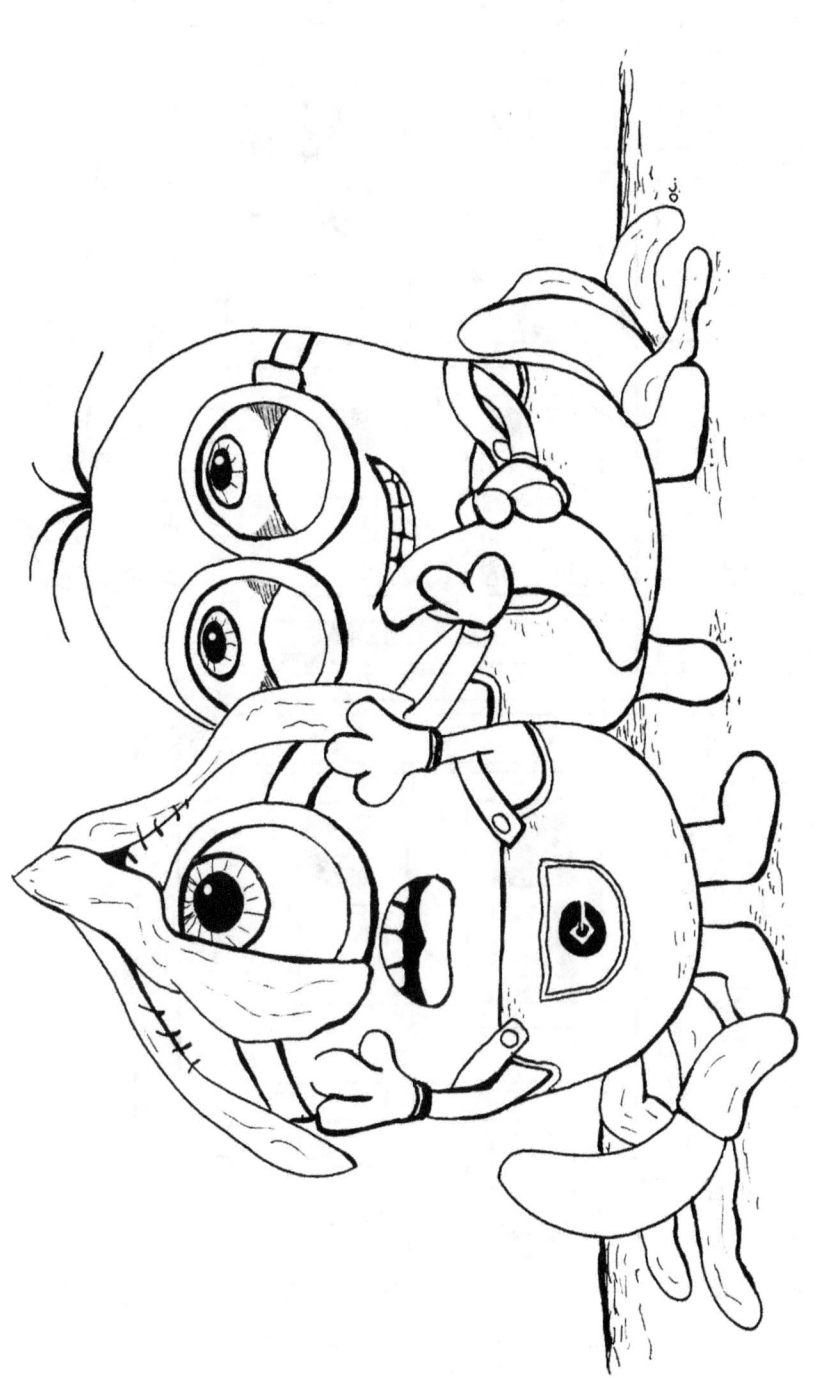

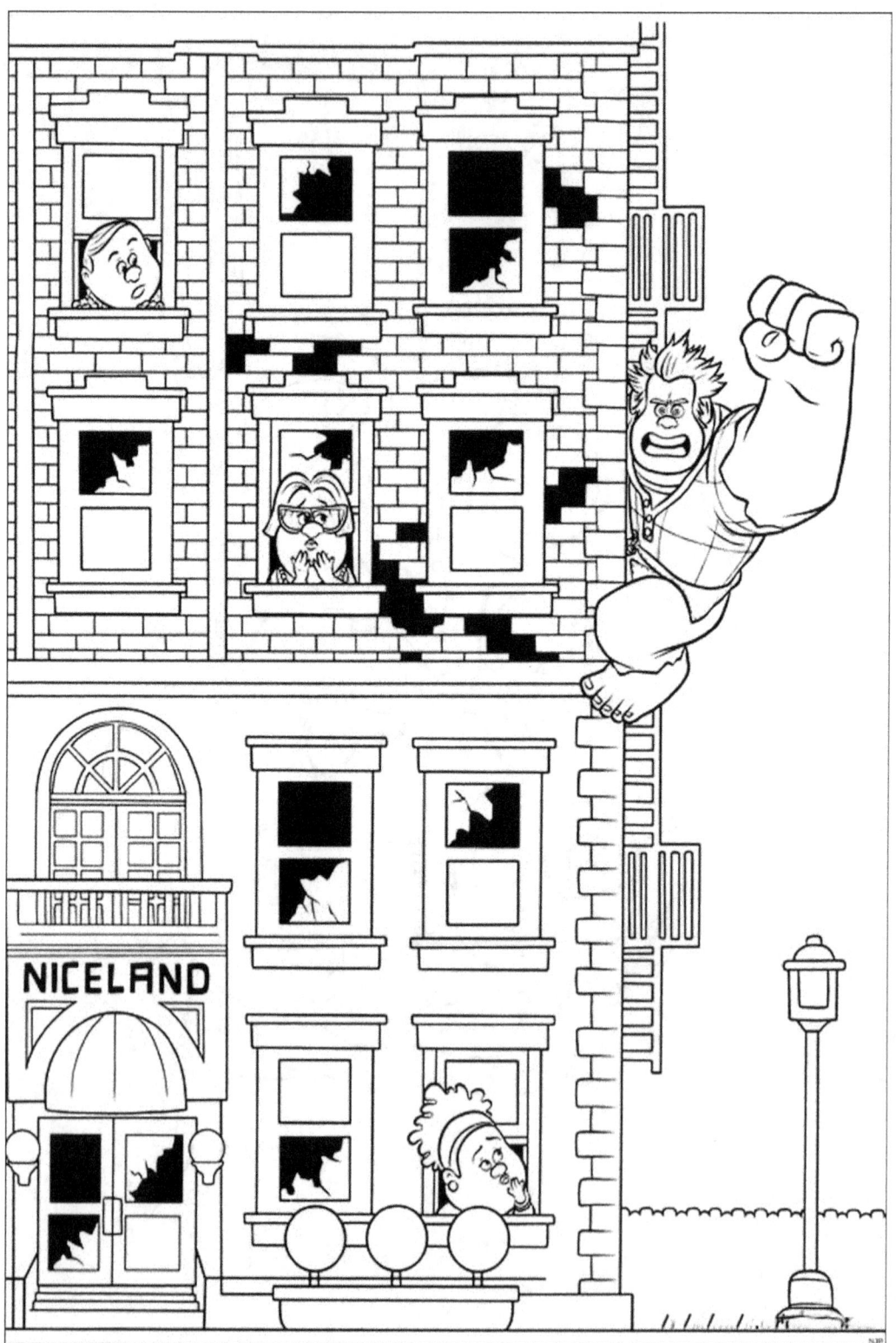

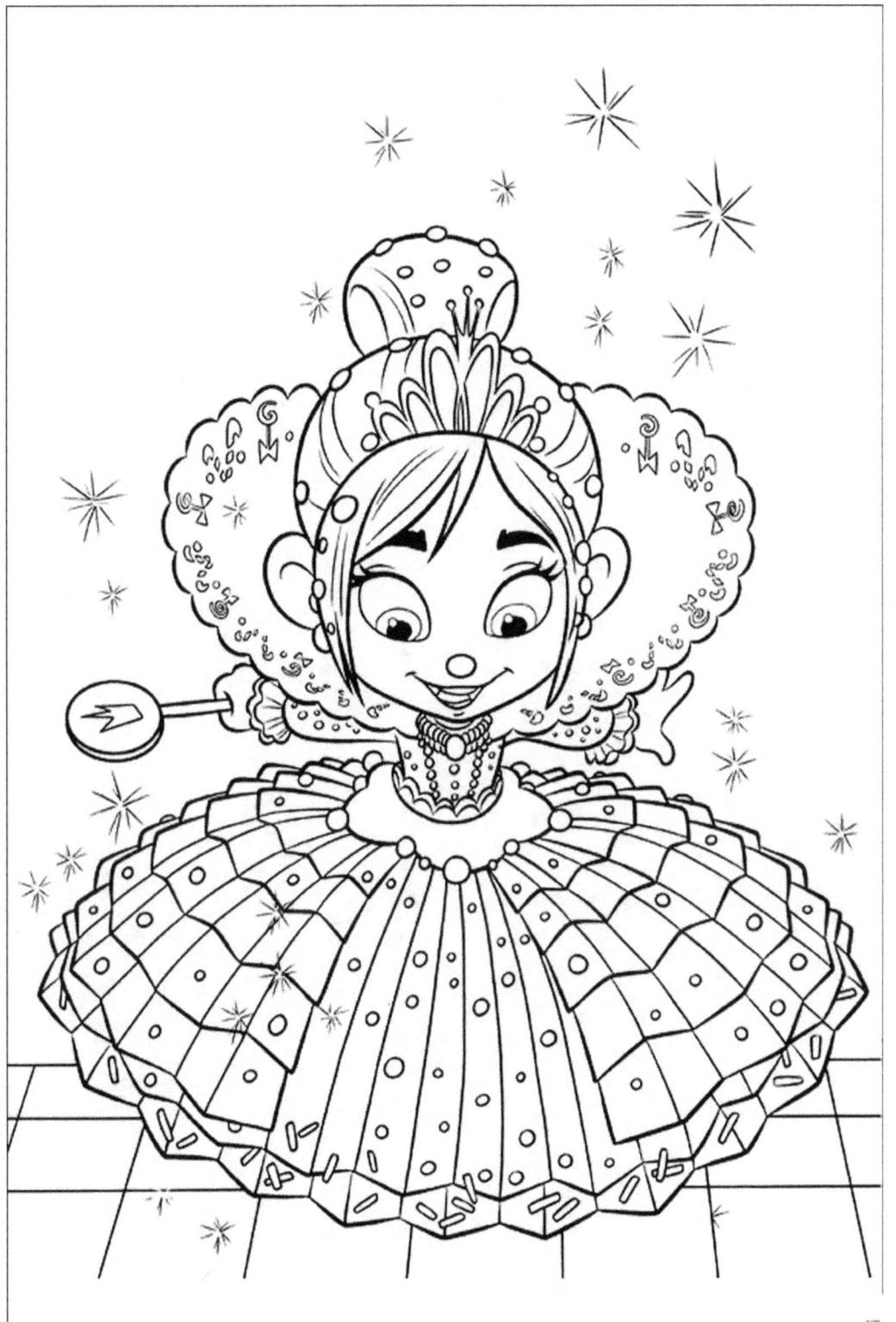

www.ingramcontent.com/pod-product-compliance
Lightning Source LLC
Chambersburg PA
CBHW070310190526
45169CB00004B/1565